**The Big Top Train is on the scene!
Everyone knows what that means!**

The circus is in town!

Let's go in and see the clowns!

Find a seat. Take your pick!

The circus dog will do a trick!

The cotton candy is so sweet.

The monkey swings by his feet!

The elephants' act is one you'll like.

The circus bear will ride his bike!

The circus is fun. Come one, come all!

Here come the lions—big and small!

Let's watch the clown. He juggles with ease!

You can have lots of treats, if you please!

The dog will catch and the monkey will throw!

Take a bow. It's the end of the show!

It's time for the circus to move to the next town.
We'll see it again when it comes back around!